Print Handwriting Workbook for Adults

Advanced Print Handwriting Worksheets with Intriguing Science Facts for a Meaningful Practice

Print Handwriting Workbook for Adults: Advanced Print Handwriting Worksheets with Intriguing Science Facts for a Meaningful Practice

Introduction to Advanced Print Handwriting

The goal of this workbook is to help you improve your print handwriting skills to an advanced level. It contains exercises for rewriting entire paragraphs and sentences (multiple times if possible). The font size is smaller compared to other standard children's practice worksheets.

This book also contains a short practice section for each letter. I recommend you complete this section first and practice each individual letter, before moving to the actual exercises. This section also includes recommendations on how each letter should be written. The rest of the workbook contains intriguing science facts from various fields like:

- *astrology*
- *anatomy*
- *physics*
- *recycling*
- *zoology*
- *and many, many more…*

At the beginning of each worksheet, you will find the sentence written in a traceable font, after that you should use the remaining space to rewrite the entire sentence again.

While I believe everyone should know how to write in cursive (because of its many scientifically proven benefits). Print handwriting doesn't go without its merits. It can help you develop a more structured and legible writing style. It is therefore important in our modern society to master both cursive and print handwriting styles. This workbook focuses on the latter.

In order to obtain the most value out of this workbook, you should not only practice your print handwriting but also improve your knowledge by learning from the short facts presented in this book. Each sentence is concise and easy to remember. Learning interesting facts from various scientific fields can help you start meaningful conversations with friends and family in your day to day life.

Print uppercase letters

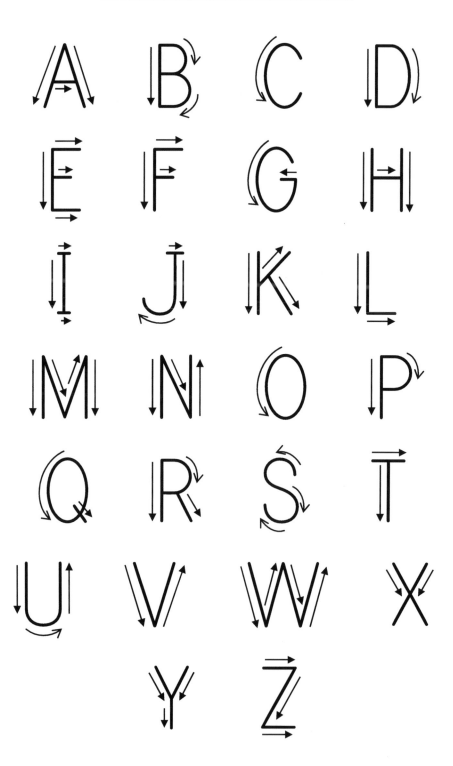

Print lowercase letters

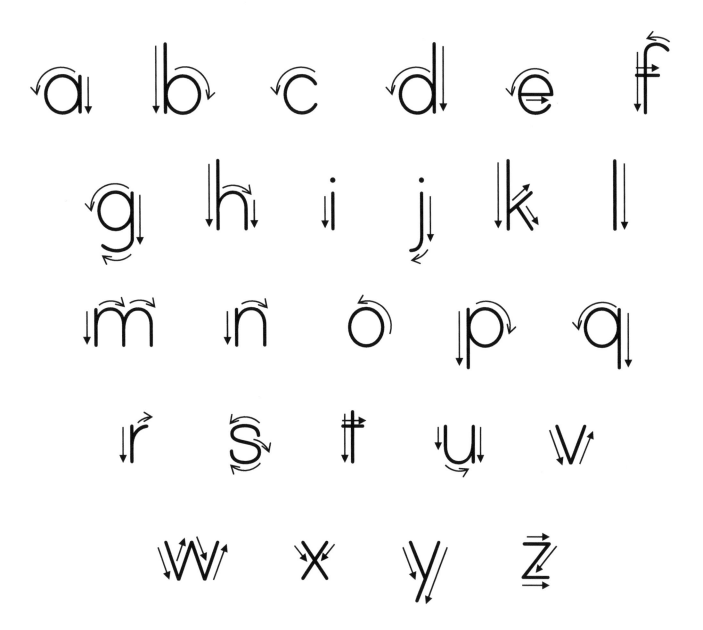

Print letter practice

H

h

I

j

J

j

K

k

l

l

M

m

N

n

O

O

P

p

Q

q

R

r

S

s

T

t

U

u

V

v

W

W

X

X

Y

Y

Z

Z

Science Fact No.1

Despite the fact that the Bobcat is the most common wildcat in America, it is rarely seen.

Despite the fact that the
Bobcat is the most common
wildcat in America, it is
rarely seen.

Science Fact No.2

Gecko feet have millions of tiny hairs that allow them to stick to surfaces with a special chemical bond.

Gecko feet have millions of
tiny hairs that allow them to
stick to surfaces with a
special chemical bond.

Science Fact No.3

The term "astronaut" comes from the Greek language and can be translated to "star" and "sailor".

The term "astronaut" comes
from the Greek language
and can be translated to
"star" and "sailor".

Science Fact No.4

While waiting for prey, the Nile crocodile can hold its breath underwater for up to two hours.

While waiting for prey, the

Nile crocodile can hold its

breath underwater for up to

two hours.

Science Fact No.5

Jellyfish have no brain, no heart and no bones.

Jellyfish have no brain, no
heart and no bones.

Science Fact No.6

A group of jellyfish is occasionally called a bloom or a swarm.

A group of jellyfish is

occasionally called a bloom

or a swarm.

Science Fact No.7

The largest salamander in the world is the Chinese giant salamander and can grow to be 6 feet (1.8 meters) long.

The largest salamander in the
world is the Chinese giant
salamander and can grow to
be 6 feet (1.8 meters) long.

Science Fact No.8

The best time to take a nap is supposedly between 1 P.M. and 2:30 P.M. due to the fact that our body experiences a dip in temperature. This, in turn, makes us feel sleepy.

The best time to take a nap
is supposedly between 1 P.M.
and 2:30 P.M. due to the fact
that our body experiences a
dip in temperature. This, in
turn makes us feel sleepy.

Science Fact No.9

In the age of the dinosaurs, a day was 23 hours long. It has changed to 24 hours because the speed of the Earth's rotation changes over time.

In the age of the dinosaurs,
a day was 23 hours long. It
has changed to 24 hours
because the speed of the
Earth's rotation changes over
time.

Science Fact No.10

The wings of a ruby-throated and rufous hummingbird can beat up to 200 times a second.

The wings of a ruby-throated
and rufous hummingbird can
beat up to 200 times a
second.

Science Fact No.11

A seahorse has the ability to move its eyes in opposite directions. This allows it to scan the water for food and predators more efficiently.

A seahorse has the ability
to move its eyes in opposite
directions. This allows it to
scan the water for food and
predators more efficiently.

Science Fact No.12

The highest wave ever surfed was 80 feet (24.3 meters) tall.

The highest wave ever surfed
was 80 feet (24.3 meters)
tall.

Science Fact No.13

Despite the fact that seahorses belong to the same class as salmon or tuna, their bodies are covered in bony plates instead of scales.

Despite the fact that
seahorses belong to the
same class as salmon or tuna,
their bodies are covered in
bony plates instead of scales.

Science Fact No.14

The name "Armadillo" means "little armored one" in Spanish.

The name "Armadillo" means
little armored one" in Spanish.

Science Fact No.15

The world smallest fruit is referred to as an
utricle and is the size of a small ant.

The world smallest fruit is
referred to as an utricle and
is the size of a small ant.

Science Fact No.16

Komodo dragons are able to consume 5 pounds
of meat in less than a minute.

Komodo dragons are able to
consume 5 pounds of meat
in less than a minute.

Science Fact No.17

In ancient times, some Viking chiefs were buried inside their ships.

In ancient times, some Viking

chiefs were buried inside

their ships.

Science Fact No.18

The Hercules beetle can grow as large as an adult human hand.

The Hercules beetle can grow
as large as an adult human
hand

Science Fact No.19

A person is able to recognize a sound in as little as 0.05 seconds.

A person is able to recognize

a sound in as little as 0.05

seconds.

Science Fact No.20

A Photon takes around 200,000 years to travel from the core of the Sun to its surface.

A Photon takes around
200,000 years to travel from
the core of the Sun to its
surface.

Science Fact No.21

Around 20% of the Earth's oxygen is produced by the Amazon rainforest.

Around 20% of the Earth's oxygen is produced by the Amazon rainforest.

Science Fact No.22

Every year, Hawaii moves 7.5 cm (2.95 inches) closer to Alaska.

Every year, Hawaii moves
7.5 cm (2.95 inches) closer
to Alaska.

Science Fact No.23

Chalk is actually made up from trillions of microscopic plankton fossils.

Chalk is actually made up
from trillions of microscopic
plankton fossils.

Science Fact No.24

Stomach acid is strong enough to dissolve metal.

Stomach acid is strong
enough to dissolve metal.

Science Fact No.25

Polar bears are experts at conserving heat and are therefore nearly undetectable by infrared cameras.

Polar bears are experts at
conserving heat and are
therefore nearly undetectable
by infrared cameras.

Science Fact No.26

A solar flare can release energy equivalent to approximately 2.5 million nuclear bombs.

A solar flare can release
energy equivalent to
approximately 2.5 million
nuclear bombs.

Science Fact No.27

Giant penguins that were about the size of a grown man existed on Earth around 59 million years ago.

Giant penguins that were
about the size of a grown
man existed on Earth around
59 million years ago.

Science Fact No.28

Contrary to popular belief, camels do not carry water in their hump. They actually carry fat.

Contrary to popular belief,
camels do not carry water in
their hump. They actually
carry fat.

Science Fact No.29

Dogs can see in color, not just in black and white. However, it is true that they can't distinguish green, red or yellow objects.

Dogs can see in color, not
just in black and white.
However, it is true that they
can't distinguish green, red
or yellow objects.

Science Fact No.30

In addition to using echolocation and despite popular belief, bats can also see.

In addition to using
echolocation and despite
popular belief, bats can also
see.

Science Fact No.31

The human tongue can actually taste any flavor
on any part of its surface.

The human tongue can
actually taste any flavor on
any part of its surface.

Science Fact No.32

People do not use only 10% of their brain. They use all of it, just not at the same time.

People do not use only 10%
of their brain. They use all of
it, just not at the same time.

Science Fact No.33

It takes about seven seconds for food to travel
down the esophagus.

It takes about seven seconds
for food to travel down the
esophagus.

Science Fact No.34

The largest internal organ is the liver. It has over
500 different functions which include fighting
infections and neutralizing toxins.

The largest internal organ is
the liver. It has over 500
different functions which
include fighting infections
and neutralizing toxins.

Science Fact No.35

At the time of this writing, around 46% of plastics are floating on the world's oceans.

At the time of this writing, around 46% of plastics are floating on the world's oceans.

Science Fact No.36

A garbage swirl the size of Texas can be found in the Pacific Ocean.

A garbage swirl the size of

Texas can be found in the

Pacific Ocean.

Science Fact No.37

At the time this was written, 100,000 marine mammals are killed each year due to plastic pollution.

At the time this was written, 100,000 marine mammals are killed each year due to plastic pollution.

Science Fact No.38

Plastic bottles require a lot more water to be produced than they can actually hold.

Plastic bottles require a lot
more water to be produced
than they can actually hold.

Science Fact No.39

Throughout the last 3000 years of civilization, there have only been 240 years of peace.

Throughout the last 3000
years of civilization, there
have only been 240 years
of peace.

Science Fact No.40

The Roman Empire was, at its height, 2.5 million square miles.

The Roman Empire was, at its
height, 2.5 million square
miles.

Science Fact No.41

Sunglasses were invented in ancient China and were used by judges in courtrooms to hide their emotions.

Sunglasses were invented in
ancient China and were used
by judges in courtrooms to
hide their emotions

Science Fact No.42

Contrary to popular belief, Napoleon was actually taller than the average Frenchman.

Contrary to popular belief,
Napoleon was actually taller
than the average Frenchman.

Science Fact No.43

Abraham Lincoln signed the Secret Service into existence on the night of his assassination.

Abraham Lincoln signed the
Secret Service into existence
on the night of his
assassination.

Science Fact No.44

In ancient Egypt, servants of the pharaoh were
smeared with honey to attract flies.

In ancient Egypt, servants of
the pharaoh were smeared
with honey to attract flies.

Science Fact No.45

Abraham Lincoln was a champion wrestler before he became a politician.

Abraham Lincoln was a

champion wrestler before

he became a politician.

Science Fact No.46

In Renaissance France, if a man was impotent, his wife could take him to court.

In Renaissance France, if a
man was impotent, his wife
could take him to court.

Science Fact No.47

In 1923, jockey Frank Hayes won a race at Belmont Park in New York after dying from a heart attack mid-race. His body stayed in the saddle until he crossed the line.

In 1923, jockey Frank Hayes

won a race at Belmont Park

in New York after dying from

a heart attack mid-race. His

body stayed in the saddle

until he crossed the line.

Science Fact No.48

Since 1945, all British tanks have included
equipment to make tea.

Since 1945, all British tanks
have included equipment to
make tea.

Science Fact No.49

Roman Emperor Gaius (known as Caligula) made
one of his favorite horses a senator.

Roman Emperor Gaius (known
as Caligula) made one of his
favorite horses a senator.

Science Fact No.50

Potatoes were introduced to Ireland in the late 1500s after being discovered by Spanish Conquistadors in Peru.

Potatoes were introduced to
Ireland in the late 1500s
after being discovered by
Spanish Conquistadors in
Peru.

Science Fact No.51

Four years before women were even given the right to vote, Jeanette Rankin became the first female member of Congress in America in 1916.

Four years before women
were even given the right to
vote, Jeanette Rankin
became the first female
member of Congress in
America in 1916.

Science Fact No.52

At the height of his popularity, Charlie Chaplin came in 20th place in a Charlie Chaplin look-a-like competition in San Francisco.

At the height of his popularity

Charlie Chaplin came in 20th

place in a Charlie Chaplin look

a like competition in San

Francisco.

Science Fact No.53

History's shortest war lasted only 38 minutes. It was between England and Zanzibar.

History's shortest war lasted
only 38 minutes. It was
between England and
Zanzibar.

Science Fact No.54

In the United States during the 1800s, it was considered a cruel punishment to feed lobster to prisoners and convicts.

In the United States during
the 1800s, it was considered
a cruel punishment to feed
lobster to prisoners and
convicts.

Science Fact No.55

Tug of War was an Olympic event between the years of 1900 and 1920.

Tug of War was an Olympic
event between the years
of 1900 and 1920.

Science Fact No.56

During the middle ages, people believed that sperm from the left testicle produced girls. To ensure having a son, some men would have their left testicle removed.

During the middle ages, people
believed that sperm from the
left testicle produced girls.
To ensure having a son,
some men would have their
left testicle removed.

Science Fact No.57

Between 1912 and 1952, the Olympics would award medals for art.

Between 1912 and 1952, the
Olympics would award medals
for art.

Science Fact No.58

In 300 B.C., turkeys were heralded by the Mayan people as vessels of the gods and were symbols of power and prestige.

In 300 B.C., turkeys were
heralded by the Mayan people
as vessels of the gods and
were symbols of power and
prestige.

Science Fact No.59

Pope Gregory IV declared war on cats in the 13th Century, claiming that black cats were instruments of Satan.

Pope Gregory IV declared war
on cats in the 13th Century,
claiming that black cats were
instruments of Satan.

Science Fact No.60

In the 1830s, ketchup was sold as medicine.

In the 1830s, ketchup was
sold as medicine.

Science Fact No.61

The first president to live in the White House
was John Adams.

The first president to live in
the White House was John
Adams.

Science Fact No.62

Karl Benz received the first patent for a gas-fueled car on January 29, 1886.

Karl Benz received the first
patent for a gas-fueled car
on January 29, 1886.

Science Fact No.63

More lifeforms are living on your skin than there are people on this planet.

More lifeforms are living on your skin than there are people on this planet.

Science Fact No.64

Leonardo da Vinci was able to write with one hand while drawing with the other.

Leonardo da Vinci was able
to write with one hand while
drawing with the other.

Science Fact No.65

The Mimic Octopus can change its color and
mimic the shapes of other animals.

The Mimic Octopus can
change its color and mimic
the shapes of other animals.

Science Fact No.66

As they transform into moths, caterpillars
completely liquify.

As they transform into moths,
caterpillars completely liquify.

Science Fact No.67

When adjusted for inflation, John D. Rockefeller is considered to be the richest man in the history of the world.

When adjusted for inflation,
John D. Rockefeller is
considered to be the richest
man in the history of the
world.

Science Fact No.68

The Northern Hemisphere is home to approximately 90% of the world's population.

The Northern Hemisphere is
home to approximately 90%
of the world's population.

Science Fact No.69

Some hummingbird species weigh less than a penny.

Some hummingbird species
weigh less than a penny.

Science Fact No.70

When the Egyptian Pyramids were being built,
the Woolly Mammoth still existed.

When the Egyptian Pyramids
were being built, the Woolly
Mammoth still existed.

Science Fact No.71

Sharks have a very acute sense of smell and can detect one part of blood in a million parts of water.

Sharks have a very acute
sense of smell and can
detect one part of blood in
a million parts of water.

Science Fact No.72

Fortune cookies are an American invention and were created by Charles Jung in 1918.

Fortune cookies are an
American invention and were
created by Charles Jung in
1918.

Science Fact No.73

The mummification process was invented by
ancient South Americans - not Egyptians.

The mummification process
was invented by ancient South
Americans - not Egyptians.

Science Fact No.74

Chocolate was consumed as early as 600 B.C.
by the Mayan civilization.

Chocolate was consumed as
early as 600 B.C. by the
Mayan civilization.

Science Fact No.75

The ancient Japanese buried people in jars
between the years of 300 B.C. and 300 A.D.

The ancient Japanese buried
people in jars between the
years of 300 B.C. and 300
A.D.

Science Fact No.76

The world's oldest temple (over 11,500 years old) is the Gobekli Tepe in Turkey.

The world's oldest temple
(over 11,500 years old) is the
Gobekli Tepe in Turkey.

Science Fact No.77

During the construction of the Great Wall of China, it is estimated that as many as 400,000 workers died.

During the construction of
the Great Wall of China, it
is estimated that as many
as 400,000 workers died.

Science Fact No.78

In ancient Egypt, men and women of similar social status were lawfully treated as equals.

In ancient Egypt, men and
women of similar social
status were lawfully treated
as equals.

Science Fact No.79

Basically, psychology is the brain trying to understand itself.

Basically, psychology is the
brain trying to understand
itself.

Science Fact No.80

Approximately 1% of the sun's mass is made up of oxygen.

Approximately 1% of the
sun's mass is made up of
oxygen.

Science Fact No.81

A single arm and a portion of the central disc of a starfish can regenerate its whole body.

A single arm and a portion of
the central disc of a starfish
can regenerate its whole
body.

Science Fact No.82

Velociraptors were actually just slightly bigger than chickens.

Velociraptors were actually just slightly bigger than chickens.

Science Fact No.83

The human brain could perform 38 thousand-trillion operations per second if it were a computer.

The human brain could

perform 38 thousand-trillion

operations per second if it

were a computer.

Science Fact No.84

Seahorses are monogamous life mates that hold each other's tails while traveling in pairs.

Seahorses are monogamous
life mates that hold each
other's tails while traveling
in pairs.

Science Fact No.85

A mosquito has a total of 47 teeth.

A mosquito has a total of 47
teeth.

Science Fact No.86

The average heart rate of a hummingbird is more than 1200 beats per minute.

The average heart rate of a
hummingbird is more than
1200 beats per minute.

Science Fact No.87

Humans share 50% of their genes with bananas (don't worry, genes only make up 2% of our DNA).

Humans share 50% of their
genes with bananas (don't
worry, genes only make up
2% of our DNA).

Science Fact No.88

The human body gives off enough heat to bring a gallon of water to boil in just 30 minutes.

The human body gives off enough heat to bring a gallon of water to boil in just 30 minutes.

Science Fact No.89

Scientific studies show that dolphins use a unique whistle to identify each other.

Scientific studies show that
dolphins use a unique whistle
to identify each other.

Science Fact No.90

Cleopatra was born closer in time to the first
moon landing than to the building of the Great
Pyramid of Giza.

Cleopatra was born closer in
time to the first moon landing
than to the building of the
Great Pyramid of Giza.

Science Fact No.91

The world's longest musical piece lasts 639 years and is being performed in the city of Halberstadt in Germany.

The world's longest musical
piece lasts 639 years and is
being performed in the city
of Halberstadt in Germany.

Science Fact No.92

Before it was actually seen through a telescope, Neptune's existence was predicted by mathematical calculations.

Before it was actually seen
through a telescope, Neptune's
existence was predicted by
mathematical calculations.

Made in the USA
Columbia, SC
09 September 2019